Tom Blower

The Humble Hero Who Conquered the North Channel

by Martin Strain

BALLYHAY BOOKS

First published by Ballyhay Books,
an imprint of Laurel Cottage Ltd.
Ballyhay, Donaghadee, N. Ireland 2019.
Copyrights Reserved.
© Text Martin Strain.
All rights reserved.
No part of this book may be reproduced or stored on any media
without the express written permission of the publishers.
Design & origination in N. Ireland.
Printed & bound by GPS Colour Graphics Ltd, Belfast
Background Bing Maps screen shots for cover reprinted with
permission from Microsoft Corporation
ISBN 978 1 910657 12 6

Foreword by
Sally Minty-Gravett MBE

As an experienced long distance and English Channel swimmer for over 45 years, which includes a two way English Channel swims in 2016 (www.swimwithsal.com), I was very honoured when on a 'wee visit' to Jersey recently, Martin asked me to read this fascinating story about the legend that is Tom Blower ... and would I consider writing a short foreword for the book? Having read the text I was delighted!

Martin started up the *Chunky Dunkers* (motto: 'Swim & eat cake') dipping group in Donaghadee, Northern Ireland in 2009 and is a very enthusiastic sea dipper and the greatest supporter of ALL North Channel swims and attempts. He is thus the ideal person to write this great account of a man's dream to achieve.

I wish Martin every success with this book; it is easy to read yet I learned so much from reading it and feel that it opens up and highlights the main challenges and difficulties of the North Channel Swim. I also know that if all North Channel Aspirants or swimmers even contemplating this tough swim, were to read this they would be approaching it with their eyes fully 'wide open' and I would urge everyone who is in training or preparing for this amazing swim, to read this as part of their preparation.

Sally Minty-Gravett[1] MBE
Jersey, Channel Islands

"Dream, achieve & inspire"

---

1. Sally Minty-Gravett is a noted long distance swimmer having conquered the English channel 7 times including a 'there and back' crossing in 2016 for which she gained recognition by the Guinness Book of Records as the oldest swimmer (59) to have achieved this feat.

Contents

Introduction

The Scottish Coast from
Donaghadee
Photo: J Hamilton

Standing below the lighthouse on the pier at Donaghadee on a clear, crisp day you feel you could almost reach out and touch the houses on the rolling hills above Portpatrick.

On such a day you might assume that the 21 miles of grey-blue waters do not seem much of a barrier, your assumption backed up by centuries of sea borne trade between the two towns. However, for the long distance swimmer this innocent stretch of water takes on a more sinister hue.

It is one of the Oceans Seven cross channel swims established in 2008 by Steven Munatones, the founder of The World Open Water Swimming Association, as the swimming equivalent of the Seven Summits mountaineering challenge. These marathon swims include the Cook Strait, the Molokai Channel, the English Channel, the Catalina Channel, the Tsugaru Strait and the Strait of Gibraltar although many would argue that none match the difficulties presented by the North Channel making it the Everest of long distance swimming.

Like climbing Everest, in recent years the North Channel swim has attracted increasing numbers willing to pit themselves against the challenge it poses. Although a significant number have succeeded, their success in no way diminishes what Tom Blower achieved in 1947.

Like the modern day climbers of Everest, although the challange is still a daunting one, the swimmers who take on the North Channel today are backed up by the latest technology in weather forecasting and navigation as well as scientifically tailored training and nutrition programmes which were unheard of in 1947.

When we are told that, to build his strength, Tom Blower had to rely on friends and relatives sharing their rations with him in the austere years following WWII you can gain some sense of how extraordinary his swim was and we can only stand back in awe at what he achieved.

By way of comparison, by the time Tom completed his epic crossing between Donaghadee and Portpatrick, the equally wide English Channel had been swum 19 times excluding several non-sanctioned crossings which were not officially recognised. Even more striking is that, in the 23 years which were to pass before anyone was able to repeat Tom's achievement, there had been some 140 officially recognised solo swims across the English Channel including several there and back double crossings.

As such Tom's triumph all those years ago should never be forgotten, no matter how many others make the crossing, or how quickly they do it. His will always have been the very first – a true pioneer in his sport!

As I'm sure you'll have gathered by now, I have always been fascinated by Tom Blower's achievements and thus when 2 old friends, Jacquie and Andy Brown, offered me the chance to view a 'scrap book' of contemporary press cuttings relating to Tom's 1947 swim, I was eager and delighted to accept.

The collection had been put together by Jacqui's Father, Jim Kimm, a Donaghadee man, who is 'recorded' as having been the engineer on the *Morning Star*, the official boat accompanying Tom during the crossing.

As I delved into the scrapbook it became clear that here was a story which needed to be told and this book is the result. If, for those with only a passing interest, I have included a little too much detail, forgive me. Please put it down to my enthusiasm for I confess that this story and indeed the stories of all who have conquered the North Channel have me enthralled!

The North Channel

Why is swimming the North Channel so difficult? What is it that makes experienced long distance swimmers call it the hardest of the Ocean 7 swim challenges?

During the summer of 2017 there were numerous attempts at swimming the North Channel, some succeeded in reaching Scotland and others didn't. One of those who successfully made the crossing was a seasoned long distance swimmer called Dean Summer. A native Australian planning to complete all of the Ocean 7 swims by the year 2020, here are his thoughts regarding the North Channel.

> "The North Channel is considered by most, the toughest of the Ocean Seven swims in that it is very cold, is plagued by the notorious Lions' Mane jellyfish and involves many competing tides and currents all the way across right up until the final few meters."

Considering each of Dean's points, first and foremost is the water temperature. Although the North Channel and the English Channel are similar in width there can be quite a difference in the water temperature. During August to September sea temperatures in the English Channel can reach a relatively comfortable 16 - 19°C. By comparison the North Channel rarely gets over 14°C with even lower temperatures in mid channel. That difference of 4 or 5°C may on the face of it not seem like a lot, but if you look at the graph left[1] (which shows predicted times for non-acclimatised people to become hypothermic when immersed in various water temperatures) you will see that between 14° and 20°, a few degrees difference in temperature can have an enormous difference on the body's ability to cope.

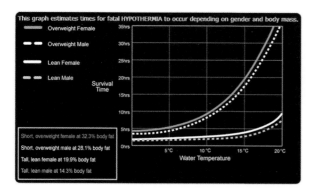

1   Courtesy of the Canadian 'Beyond Cold Water Bootcamp' website http://www.beyondcoldwaterbootcamp.com

Of course these graphs are for 'average' people rather than those who have spent years acclimatising their bodies for the hardships of cold water swimming. However, given that most of those who undertake this swim will be in the water for anything between 12 and 18 hours, even one or two degrees difference in the water temperature can mean the difference between success and failure.

To aid swimmers in the battle against the cold they routinely plaster their bodies, from head to foot, in what they refer to as a 'channel grease mix' although its merits are disputed. Tracy Clark a highly respected long distance swimmer had this to say:

> "Grease is a personal choice. I slather on Vaseline in all my chafe spots, under arms, on shoulders, under swim straps, around the neck and under the chin. There is a myth that Lanolin/Grease/Vaseline keeps you warm. Nothing keeps you warm except for a layer of good healthy brown fat!""

The second difficulty Dean Summers refers to is jellyfish. Ireland has 5 indigenous species of jellyfish and unfortunately for swimmers, it is the largest species of jellyfish in the world, the Lions Mane, which is both the most common (and the most dangerous) species in the North Channel. When attempting this crossing it's not really a question of 'if' you are going to get stung, it's a question of 'when' will it happen.

There are numerous accounts of swimmers getting stung by Lions Mane jellyfish and whilst they had to endure hours of agony, they remained perfectly capable of continuing their swim. Other swimmers however, weren't so fortunate as the online account of long distance swimmer Edward Williams's first attempt at the North Channel in October 2014 illustrates. Williams tells how after 18 months of hard training his swim was brought to an untimely and terrifying end by his body's reaction to literally hundreds of Lions Mane stings. Of his first encounter he says:

> "Within 5 minutes I felt a familiar jolt of pain to my face and arms. It was like a net of acid covering me which was quickly spreading to every cell of my skin. I had swum straight into my first Lions Mane jellyfish."

Lion's Mane jellyfish, Cyanea capillata

Continuing he recounts how throughout the swim he was:

> "constantly banging into them and being stung … Each sting was like a shot of agony … I could feel their tentacles clinging to me and could feel them pulsing their venom into me, which was really unnerving as well as agonising."

Stung on his body, his face and even inside his mouth. Williams started to vomit and experienced severe respiratory difficulties. By this point he was only 4 miles short of his goal and with Scotland tantalisingly close he continued swimming for as long as he could until he suddenly lost the power in his stroke and his muscles began to spasm. Realising that this situation was becoming life threatening, he and his team rightly decided it was time to stop – truly harrowing!

The third difficulty raised by Dean which faces any North Channel swimmer is the strength and speed of the tides which race through between Northern Ireland and Scotland.

In very simple terms, in time with the tide, water flows in and out of the Irish sea through the St. George's and the North Channels. As the tide comes in, the water between Donaghadee and Portpatrick flows in a southerly direction for around 6 hours, before it 'ebbs out' in a northerly direction, for another 6 hours, back from whence it came. Then the cycle begins again. Of course the tides do not flow in and out uniformly because when water flows through a constriction, i.e. between a mainland and an island or an outcrop of rocks, 'tidal eddies' are set up which result in strong circular currents of water. Only people with local knowledge will know of their locations and for swimmers that knowledge is priceless.

Given that a channel swimmer will be in the water for 12-18 hours, all these currents pushing them hither and thither adds extra distance to the length of the swim and, because of this, the ideal time to make an attempt is when the currents are weakest.

The strength of the currents produced by the tidal flow fluctuate due to several factors. Most importantly their strength is greatest when the difference between high and low tide is largest (spring tide) and weakest when difference between high and low tide is least (neap tide).

To complete the North Channel swim without facing impossible currents, there is only a very brief 'window of opportunity' lasting a day or two either side of the neap tide which occurs twice a month. A successful crossing also requires good weather and given the unpredictable weather in the North channel, the scarcity of tidal windows which coincide with favourable weather means swimmers are often forced to embark on their journey when either the tides or the weather is less than perfect.

These three factors alone: the cold; the jellyfish; the currents, would cement the North Channel's position as the toughest of the Oceans 7 swim challenges – and that's not even mentioning that it's a 21 mile swim!

Perhaps the best summary of the difficulties facing the North Channel swimmer that I've seen, is the following paragraph lifted from a 1963 copy of the world renowned *Sports Illustrated* magazine:

> "From Donaghadee in Northern Ireland to Portpatrick in Scotland is a fraction less than 21 miles. Between the two land masses the sea rages in swollen tides and hungry eddies. Out in the centre a man could sink some 100 fathoms in places before touching the dark bottom. The water is so painfully cold that to swim in it is to feel as if one has a steel band around his forehead that gets tighter with each stroke. This is the deadly and cruel North Channel of the Irish Sea. To long-distance swimmers it makes the English Channel look like a wading pond. Only one swimmer has ever made it across – an Englishman named Tom Blower."

Mercedes Glietz

Mercedes Glietz discussing the swim with the Author's great-grandfather, Dan Davidson

Prior to WWII there appears to be very little on record regarding any attempts to swim the North Channel aside from the efforts of the famous and glamorous English open water swimmer Mercedes Gleitze.

Born in Brighton on the 18th of November 1900, Mercedes was the youngest of 3 daughters to German immigrants Heinrich and Anna. As a child she was taught to swim by her father and what began as a hobby soon became a lifelong obsession with the sport.

By the time she was in her twenties she had secured employment as a stenographer in London and any spare time she had was spent swimming in the River Thames where, in 1923, she completed a record breaking 27-mile swim.

On the 7th October 1927 displaying a level of perseverance and dogged determination which would become her hallmark, she became the first British woman to successfully swim the English Channel after no less than 7 unsuccessful attempts.

Entering the water in France at 2:55am Mercedes bravely battled her way through the dark murky seas, which were shrouded in heavy fog. Visibility was very poor, at times reduced to less than 5 yards as she courageously swam on. Then at 6:10pm, some 15 hours and 15 minutes after entering the water, her 'feet touched the chalk rocks between South Foreland and St Margaret's Bay.' Mercedes struggled ashore before collapsing unconscious into the arms of her trainer, remaining unconscious for almost two hours.

Buoyed by the success of swimming the English Channel Mercedes quickly moved on to yet another challenge; The 14.5 km swim across the Straits of Gibraltar, from Spain to Morocco.

Her first attempt on the 16th December ended unsuccessfully when she was forced out of the water after 8 hours due to stormy conditions. However, showing typical Gleitze perseverance, after four further unsuccessful attempts she eventually succeeded and on the 5th April 1928 she became the first swimmer to conquer the Straits of Gibraltar.

Never one to let the grass grow under her feet, Mercedes quickly focused her attention on yet another challenge. In early May she announced in numerous newspapers that her next big swim would be the North Channel, from Portpartick to Donaghadee.

Mercedes appointed as her manager for the swim a Mr Hugh Muir, a native of Portpatrick who some decades previously had served alongside Donaghadee man James Davidson on the *SS Terrible* carrying mail and passengers on the route between Donaghadee and Portpatrick. On being appointed as Mercedes' manager Muir sought Davidson's advice and it's recorded that it was from these contacts that the decision was made to commence the Channel swims from Donaghadee rather than Portpatrick as was originally planned.

With everything in place on 4 separate occasions during 1928: Saturday 23rd June; Thursday 26th July; Sunday 26th August; and Monday 5th November, Mercedes set out from Donaghadee fully prepared and determined to swim to Portpatrick.

The narrative of each of the unsuccessful attempts is very similar: Mercedes would start each swim strongly, using mostly breaststroke, and make good headway in the early stages. However, it appears that she wasn't quite prepared for the wickedly cold temperatures of the North Channel and as the cold drained her reserves her efforts would falter.

Of her first swim which took place on Saturday 23rd June, the *Sheffield Daily Telegraph* records that 7¾ hours later she had to be pulled from the water into the pilot's skiff completely exhausted and bemused. Muttering about the water temperature Mercedes said *"it's terrible!"* and her legs were paralysed! Interviewed later the swimmer related that at one point near the centre of the channel the temperature had dropped to 40 degrees farenheit.

Mercedes second attempt took place on Thursday 26th July. As on her first arrival in Donaghadee, she received what the *News Letter* 25th July describes as an 'Enthusiastic Welcome.' by large crowds of locals. Such was the level of attention Mercedes received; she was forced into leaving her hotel, The Royal, to seek solitude and rest in a quiet country house at Ballywilliam, just outside the town. Mercedes entered the water at 2:50am and as the *Sheffield Daily Telegraph* records, *'despite the early hour, thousands of people were present.'* The water temperature was slightly kinder on this occasion, up to 51 farenheit. Again, however it was the biting cold which forced Mercedes to abandon the swim.

August 26th saw Mercedes back to Donaghadee for her third attempt. Prior to her swim she had the pleasant task of bestowing her name *'Mercedes'* on the newly acquired motor boat of yet another well known Donaghadee man involved in piloting her swims, Andy White. A man who would later be a key player in Tom Blower's efforts.

Once again the water temperature had improved a little, this time up to 56 farenheit and Mercedes was able to stay in the water for longer than for any of her other attempts, commencing swimming at 5:25am and continuing until almost 9:30pm – 16 hours! As in her previous attempts Mercedes' boat crew had played gramophone music and sang to her as she was swimming. One reporter in the *Aberdeen Press and Journal* records the end of this 3rd attempt in these words:

> "One of her attendants on the launch told a Press reporter that the last minutes of Miss Gleitze's swim were pathetic. Her doctor and others on board had repeatedly entreated her to give up the effort, but she persisted carrying on, and finally had to be lifted from the water. She appeared be in a helpless condition."

Mercedes however is quoted in the *Birmingham Daily Gazette* as saying, *"I shall never give it up,"*

Thus on the afternoon of the 5th November, Mercedes once again entered the waters of the North Channel.

In a confident frame of mind despite her pilot, Andrew White, having advised her that "her chance of accomplishing much more than five miles was very remote" since the sea would gradually become worse once she was clear of the Copeland Islands.

Mercedes choose to ignore his advice deciding to go anyway and using a steady breast stroke she was again seen off by a large crowd of well-wishers. With a gramophone playing she struck out in almost perfect conditions covered from head to toe in olive oil and lard in an effort to protect her from the cold.

However she should have paid more heed to her pilot's local knowledge as conditions soon deteriorated.

The *News Letter* records the finale in these words:

> "At seven o'clock Miss Gleitze called out to her pilot, Andrew White, and with great difficulty managed to say, "The cold is terrible. It is killing me. Will people understand if I give up?" At 7pm she was dragged into the boat barely conscious and blue with the cold."

At a later interview Mercedes said:

> "I endured acute pain. The wind cut through my chest like a knife and benumbed my limbs. I fought vainly to shake it off. I did my best but the conditions were too bad. This is the last attempt this year."

The *Northern Whig* on the 6th November records that:

> "Mercedes was naturally disappointed at the outcome of her venture, but realised that she had attempted impossibility."

Displaying her trademark dogged determination Mercedes returned to the North Channel again the following year this time starting from the Scottish side. However, after a further four unsuccessful attempts, she finally admitted defeat.

Tom Blower, Early Days

The story of Tom Blower's North Channel swim from Donaghadee to Portpatrick on the 27th July 1947 starts not in Donaghadee, but way back in his home town of Nottingham where he was born into a mining family in the working class Hysen Green area of Nottingham on the 16th January 1914.

Although his swimming exploits would eventually see him nicknamed 'Torpedo Tom', he knew exactly where his strengths lay and it was not in racing but in distance swimming – indeed Tom described himself as a 'cart horse' due to his lack of speed in the sprint swimming races.

His Mother made this observation about the young Tom:

"Ever since my boy began swimming as a schoolboy of eight, and all through his career, he has had the idea of a cross channel attempt in mind....he is a quiet lad but one of the most conscientious in the world. He never rests once he gets his mind set on an idea!"

Proving that this was not just a proud mother's idle boast, by the time he was 21, Tom's distance swimming prowess had progressed to the point where he became the first non-Lancastrian, to win the ten mile race across Morecambe Bay. According to the *Lancashire Evening Post* he was the only one to finish from a field which, although few in number, included a three time previous winner.

Two years later on the 4th August 1937, Tom at age 23 became a world record holder, when he swam the English Channel in 13 hours 29 minutes.

MORECAMBE BAY HIS SECOND SEA SWIM

Nottingham Youth the Only One to Finish

OTHERS STRANDED

THOUSANDS of holiday-makers lining Morecambe Central Promenade on Saturday saw a lone swimmer reach the fore-shore after a 12-mile struggle with currents, tricky tides, and waves, and a gun-shot signified that at his first attempt he had won the first cross-bay swim of the season promoted by the Morecambe Cross-Bay Swimming Association.

He was Thomas W. Blower, a 21-year-old tobacco worker from Nottingham, who had only swum in the sea once before—last week at Skegness—and until recently had never swum further than two miles. His time was 3hr. 5min. 30sec., and he was the only one to finish out of five entrants, the others being stranded on a mudbank half-way across.

The unsuccessful competitors were Charles Daly, Manchester, three times winner of the cross-bay championship; Alan Gorton, the 16-year-old Failsworth swimmer, the youngest boy to ever swim the bay; Sidney Moss, Hyde, a previous entrant; and Arthur Darch, of Nottingham, who had recently been residing at Heit Bank, and who entered last year.

Lancashire
Evening Post
5th August
1935

17

Nottingham Journal

LATE CITY EDITION

NOTTINGHAM MAN BREAKS THE CHANNEL OFFICIAL RECORD
Knocks One Hour Off Temme's Time Yet Feels Fresher Than When He Started!

"Human Torpedo" May Make Bid for Both-ways Crown

WIFE'S "BLESS YOU, TOM" GREETING

OLD MAN OF THE SEA GRINS, "HE CAN DO IT AGAIN!"

NOTTINGHAM HERO No. 1

SWIMMING HISTORY OF TOM BLOWER

LIFE'S AMBITION

MOTHER SAYS " HE IS A QUIET LAD"!

In an earlier interview with the *Nottingham Journal* printed on the 5th August 1937 Tom's mother said:

> As a boy he used to look at the picture of Capt. Webb on the match boxes and he would say "I might swim the channel some day, mam"... "and you might not" I used to reply.

While Tom may have fulfilled his ambitions in the English Channel he had a bigger goal in mind as revealed in an interview with his father by the *Nottingham Evening Post*:

TOM BLOWER HOPES TO TACKLE IRISH CHANNEL

> Tom Blower's greatest ambition iin life is to swim the Irish Channel, a feat never yet accomplished. This facet was revealed by Blower's father last night, after he had heard the news of his son's success in swimming the English Channel.
>
> "If there is enough money left and he is given a week's rest he will try and swim the English Channel the other way, and when he has done that he will want to swim the Irish Channel" was almost Mr Blower's first comment.
>
> "He has had this Irish Channel swim in his head for a long time – and he'll do it if he can get enough money."

As well as the statement of intent regarding the North Channel, it is interesting to note that Tom's father twice refers to money, which would seem to indicate it was in limited supply. However, despite the successes Tom achieved, there seems to be no evidence that he ever had any desire to turn professional as he always stated that he swam for pleasure and cherished his amateur status highly. Perhaps his father's words were just parental concerns about the financial strains (time off work, travel, hire of pilots etc) such an attempt would place on his son's new family.

Tom had married in June 1936 and in September 1938 his wife Clarice gave birth to their only child, a son Michael. However marriage, or indeed the pending birth of his son, appears not to have had any unfavourable impact on his swimming prowess if we are to believe the following report from 1938:

> Tom Blower, the Nottingham swimmer, swam across Morecambe Bay so swiftly on Saturday that the pilot rowing boat could hardly keep pace. The pilots had to row so hard that they were exhausted at the finish whilst the swimmer was as fresh as a daisy. Blower's time, 2 hours 55 minutes was the best for six years and it is expected he will retain the championship with it. The Barrow Town Councillor, J. H. Brown finished in an exhausted state the eleven miles course from Grange to Morcambe in three hours 28 minutes but H. Bracewell (Blackpool) and Miss K. E. Hodgson (Grange), last year's lady champion, both gave up through cramp.
>
> Nottingham Journal 29th August 1938

Although Tom's reputation as a swimmer was growing by the end of the decade storm clouds were gathering and his life, along with the lives of millions of others across the world, was turned upside down with the outbreak of the Second World War.

Given his association with the sea it was almost inevitable that as the country's young men were called to war, Tom would enlist with the Royal Navy where he served for five and a half years. This included a stint on the Royal Navy Flower Class Corvette, CANDYTUFT which operated from Londonderry and saw action in the Battle of the Atlantic. Typical activities would have included protecting convoys and searching for/attacking German U-boats, which at that time were wreaking havoc among Allied ships and convoys.

CANDYTUFT's service was not without incident and Tom was part of the crew on the 9th September 1941 in the North Atlantic when she suffered a boiler explosion killing 11 of the ship's crew.

HMS Candytuft

On another occasion one of Tom's shipmates had cause to be thankful for Tom's swimming prowess after he ended up in the water following a dive-bombing attack. Tom jumped into the Atlantic to rescue his stricken comrade and for this act of valour he was awarded a Royal Humane Society Medal.

When victory was finally achieved, Tom returned to Nottingham where he resumed working for the Nottingham based tobacco company, John Player and Sons with whom he had worked as a mechanic before the War. However rather than as a mechanic this time he was employed as an advertising agent – clearly the views on links between tobacco and health in the 1950s were somewhat different than today!

On Thursday 20th June 1946, Tom returned to competitive swimming for the first time since coming home after the war, although on this occasion, as was reported the next evening, it wasn't a long distance swim that he participated in. It was in fact a water polo match for his home team, Nottingham S.C., against Burton. His return was not an auspicious one as Nottingham lost 5:4 but the report makes clear that Tom's sights were still set on conquering the North Channel even if the accuracy of some of the details leave something to be desired!

SMOKE PLAYER'S NAVY CUT TOBACCO AND CIGARETTES

BLOWER'S RETURN.

Mr. T. Lewin, of the Nottingham S.C., took water polo and swimming team to Burton-on-Trent last night for a friendly match against combined Burton team …

… This was Tommy Blower's first appearance since the war in competitive swimming. Nottingham's famous English Channel and Morecambe Bay swimmer has expressed a wish to make an attempt to swim from England to Ireland. He feels pretty confident that he would be able to become the first to accomplish the feat —he would be the first to attempt it – providing suitable backing could be found

The Nottingham Evening Post 21/6/1946

Tom Blower

Less than a month after he had made his return to competitive swimming Tom announced that he had decided to follow up on the ambitions alluded to after his successful pre-war English Channel swim, with an attempt at the North Channel as reported in a short statement in *The Nottingham Evening Post*, dated 12th July 1946:

TOM BLOWER AND IRISH CHANNEL.

Tom Blower, the Nottingham Channel swimmer, is about to commence training for the attempt the Irish Channel, which he proposes make during his holidays.

With the attempt planned for the summer of 1947, Tom was giving himself a full year to prepare for what would be the toughest swim of his life – a year to train and build himself up physically and mentally to tackle one of the biggest challenges in swimming.

And a year would be needed, not only to get Tom prepared, but to actually establish what he was going to attempt. There are numerous contemporary newspaper cuttings reporting on Tom's plans to swim the channel. All of them including *The Dundee Evening Telegraph, The Lancaster Guardian, The Londonderry Sentinel and The Staffordshire Advertiser,* make it abundantly clear that the initial intention was to make the crossing not between Donaghadee and Portpatrick, but between Larne and Stranraer!

…In his record English Channel swim he was fed every hour, yet lost seven pounds in weight. He is now looking ahead rather ruefully and wondering how the 15oz. ration of bread he gets as manual worker will serve him in the longer crossing to Ireland. No route has been fixed for the attempt, but a friend has suggested Stranraer-Larne. Tom's employers, Messrs. John Player and Sons, have allowed him extra time during his holidays next year for the attempt.

Nottingham Journal 13th July 1946

...Tom Blower, 32-year-old Nottingham swimmer, four times Morecambe Bay cross-swim champion, is to try to swim 30 miles across the Irish Sea from Larne to Stranraer. Mr Jock Mount, a Morecambe fisherman, who mapped a course In 1939, when the suggestion was first made, is making arrangements for the swim some time next summer

Lancashire Evening Post 19th November 1946

... After six years in the Navy, Tom Blower of Nottingham, English Channel swimmer and Morecambe cross-Bay champion, is going into training to swim the Irish Sea from Larne to Stranraer, a distance of 30 miles, next summer. He will have as his trainer Morcambe veteran fisherman Jack Mount, who has had long experience of the Irish Sea as a yachtsman.

Dundee Evening Telegraph 19th November 1946

... Tom Blower, the Nottingham Channel swimmer, is working hard in preparation for his attempt to swim the Irish Channel from Stranraer to Larne, next July. He is swimming for several hours as often as he can, and some judges aver that he is best long distance swimmer in the country, and probably the world. To help him in his training, the Nottingham S.C. would like to secure the services of a few performers swim along with Blower.

Nottingham Evening Post, 2nd April 1947

Even the most fleeting glance at a map would show the folly of this plan. The distance between Donaghadee to Portpatrick is 21 miles whereas from Larne to the nearest point in Scotland is some 25 miles. To then swim round the head of the Mull of Galloway and down Lough Ryan to get to Stranraer adds another 15 miles for a total distance of some 40 miles!

It's hard to believe that Tom would have ever seriously considered such a route, so why it was suggested let alone printed unchallenged and without explanation in so many newspapers is not clear. Perhaps it was that 'Larne – Stranraer', being the ferry route, would have better recognition among an English readership or perhaps it was simply an early example of 'Fake News'. Certainly, by April Tom's support team had already made contact with individuals in Portpatrick and Donaghadee seeking their assistance. Whatever the reason it was not until June 1947, just a few weeks before the swim was due to take place that the *Nottingham Evening Post* reported:

Tom's 16-hour swim is part of the preparation for his attempt to swim 22 miles of the Irish Channel from Donaghadee in Co. Down to Portpatrick, near Stranraer – a feat which has never been accomplished

Of course, before he could consider swimming any route across the North Channel Tom had to get himself into shape for the challenge. To reach the level of fitness and endurance required would be a daunting task at the best of times but for a working class man living through the austere days immediately following WWII there were additional obstacles to be overcome.

Despite the war having been won, in 1946/47 rationing was still very much in place. Although the wartime diet was actually quite high in calories they were mostly sourced from starchy carbohydrates. Proteins and fats which today would be considered essential to get an athlete built up for a long distance swim were in short supply.

Fortunately Tom was not without friends and supporters and the following cutting sheds light on how they helped:

> ... Mrs. Blower, making her second trip with her husband on a Channel swim – she accompanied him when he swam the English Channel in 1937 – paid tribute to the many friends who gave extra rations in helping bring Tom's strength, and energy to its highest pitch, for a man cannot train for Channel swim on present-day rations alone, "Our friends have been very good us in this way," she said ...
>
> The Nottingham Evening Post 3rd July 1947

The importance of this facet of Tom's preparation was highlighted subsequently by at least one of those who made laudatory speeches to Tom whilst celebrating his success in the Donaghadee Town Hall. He said that Tom owed his wife a great debt as he would never have been able to complete the swim, had it not been for his wife, Clarice, standing in the queue at shops to collect his rations!

With diet taken care of, Tom was able to focus on his swimming. As mentioned earlier his mother had testified that her son was *"a quiet lad but one of the most conscientious in the world. He never rests once he gets his mind set on an idea"* and thus Tom embarked on a gruelling training programme that was well covered in the local newspapers at the time.

Finally, like anything in life, a certain amount of money would be needed to finance the swims. At the time the estimated figure was £400-£500; not an insubstantial sum given that the average working wage was less than £300 per anum.

BLOWER'S SKEGNESS SWIMS

Two Hours in Pool: Three in Sea

TOM BLOWER did two training swims at Skegness yesterday.

Although the weather was definitely on the cold side, and the temperature of the water down to 59 degrees, some 400 people assembled at the Bathing Pool in the afternoon to watch the Nottingham marathon swimmer.

Tom and his trainer, Mr. C. E. Cragg arrived at the resort about noon, and after a meal, Tom entered the water at 3 o'clock and spent two hours non-stop swimming up and down the pool, covering in all about 4½ miles.

His easy rhythmic stroke provoked much admiring comment from the onlookers, who included visitors from all parts of the country and his tireless action was well summed up by one who remarked: "He looks as if he could go on for ever, like Tennyson's Brook."

TO INGOLDMELS

After leaving the pool, Mr. Cragg accompanied Blower to the sea. where the swimmer waded into the water, and in the presence of several hundred more spectators, swam about a mile out and then headed north for a long, straight swim to opposite Ingoldmels Point Here he turned back and later stepped out of the water apparently as fresh as when he entered it after a three-hours' swim, during which he covered approximately 6½ miles.

Tom, who with his trainer returned to Nottingham last evening, will again visit Skegness next Sunday for a repeat training performance.

Nottingham Journal 16th June

15 HOURS IN THE SEA

Tom Blower Trains at Mablethorpe

THOUSANDS of holidaymakers at Mablethorpe over the week-end were unaware that practising for his forthcoming attempt on the North Channel was 33-year-old Tom Blower, of Nottingham.

Blower arrived at Mablethorpe with his wife and child on Friday night and told a "Journal" representative on Saturday morning of his plans. He unobtrusively entered the sea on Saturday afternoon and swam for about three hours. In the evening he put in some more practice, accompanied by his trainer, Mr. C. E. Grabb.

Practice intensified yesterday, when he spent three hours in the water and two out, and he put it: "Getting myself well pickled in sea water."

His trainer is confident that his attempt will be successful. After spending some 15 hours in the water, Tom and his party returned by car to Nottingham late last night.

Nottingham Journal 23rd June

TOM BLOWER AT MABLETHORPE

When interviewed by a "Journal" representative at Mablethorpe on Saturday, Nottingham's Channel swimmer, Tom Blower, was putting himself on the right side of a particularly large dinner.

"All I want now is plenty of good food," he said, and in this he was backed up by his trainer, Mr. C. E. Cragg, of Nottingham.

Down at Mablethorpe to complete his training for his attempt on the North Channel, Blower described the place as "ideal."

Together with Mr. C. G. Dulson, of Nottingham, and his trainer, Blower arrived at Mablethorpe by car on Friday night and spent three periods of nearly two hours each in the sea. He returned to Nottingham last night.

Thousands of visitors watched the practice swims.

Nottingham Journal 30th June

Again Tom's friends rallied round and a small committee was formed to help with funding the swim. This included Nottingham businessmen, Councillors and friends who also helped with all the practicalities involved. Tom's long term employers, Players Tobacco, were also a great supporter during this period, as he trained and prepared for his swim. Fund raising efforts were made to facilitate Tom in his efforts including Swimming Galas and Exhibitions in and around the Nottingham and Morecambe areas.

Chairman of the Tom Blower Fund Committee was Alderman R E Ashworth but many of the arrangements regarding the logistics of the swim seem to have been made by the committee's secretary, Mr J T Grundy.

Old Naval Comrades

Aid Tom Blower's Swim Expenses

IT was only at the close of last night's meeting of the Nottingham branch of the Royal Naval Old Comrades' Association in the Spread Eagle Hotel that a member called attention to Tom Blower's coming attempt to swim the Irish Channel.

It was immediately and unanimously resolved to forward a cheque for five guineas to help defray his expenses which are estimated at between £400 and £500.

Tom Blower is himself a member of the Nottingham branch of the association and when he goes over to Ireland he will carry with him a letter from his fellow shipmates of Nottingham wishing him every success

It was reported that Ald. E A. Braddock would be visiting them at next month's meeting to invite members to visit the training ship "Orion" on the banks of the Trent.

Nottingham Journal 2nd July 1947

Final Plans for Irish Sea Swim

THE committee which is organising Tom Blower's swim across the Irish Channel assembled at the Victoria Baths, Nottingham, last night to complete the arrangements.

The party will leave for Ireland on 4 July, and will stay at Donaghadee, near Bangor, where Tom will make a few short training swims before the major attempt on the first favourable day between 10 and 14 July.

"We are confident that given satisfactory weather conditions, Blower will succeed in being the first man to register a notch for Great Britain, Ald. R. E. Ashworth, chairman of the committee, told the "Journal."

"On the Irish side they are very enthusiastic and the civic authorities are very keen on the swim." he added.

This week-end Tom Blower will make his last training swim on the English side at Mablethorpe.

Dr I. R. Spark, a member of the committee, will travel up to Port Patrick in Scotland when the attempt is made and he hopes to charter a boat and meet Tom half way across.

Nottingham Journal
26th June 1947

It would appear that Mr Grundy's initial research led him to Portpatrick where he was advised to contact Mr W H Roberts in Donaghadee to seek his advice and assistance.

Mr Roberts owned the gasworks in the town and his motor launch, *The Kathleen*, had been used by Mercedes Gleitze in her unsuccessful attempts to swim the North Channel in 1928. With this experience behind him as well as being an important business man in Donaghadee, Mr Roberts was a potentially invaluable contact for Tom's team. Fortunately for them, from the moment he was contacted Mr Roberts seems to have made every effort to assist as noted by Mr Grundy in a later letter on the 6th August where he thanked him for:

…the excellent and sporty way in which you came to our assistance as soon as we approached you on this matter.

As can be seen from Mr Grundy's April letter, Tom's team required a Pilot, a pilot boat and accommodation for Tom and his entourage for the duration.

It is interesting to note that Tom's team seem to have been unaware of Donaghadee's position as a pre-eminent holiday destination which, during July, would have been bursting at the seams

GENERAL MANAGER &

ALL COMMUNICATIONS TO BE ADDRESSED TO "GENERAL SUPERINTENDENT."

TELEPHONE No. 41907

JTG/DB.

General Superintendent's Office.
Baths & Wash-houses Dept.,
Victoria Baths.
Sneinton. **Nottingham.**
10th. April 1947.

J. T. GRUNDY, M.N.A.B.S
GENERAL SUPERINTENDENT —

Mr. W.H. Roberts,
Gas Works House,
Donaghadee,
County Antrim, N. Ireland.

Dear Sir,

In Nottingham we have a well known Swimmer named Tom Blower. On 4th. August 1937, he swam the English Channel in 13 hours 29 minutes. During the war Tom served in the Royal Navy for over 5½ years, finishing as a Petty Officer. He is 6' 1" and weighs 17 stone. Now his ambition is to swim from Ireland to Scotland.

Mr. James McMaster of "Braefield", Portpatrick gave me your address and I am writing to see if you can assist us in any way. Mr. McMaster told me of the big part you played in the attempts made by Miss M. Gleize in 1928 and 1929.

A Committee has been formed in Nottingham to further the Swim and I have been appointed Secretary and Organiser. It is hoped that the attempt will be made on or about the 13th. July.

You could help us greatly if you could inform me of a suitable Pilot who knows the run of the waters in those parts. Also, could you kindly let me know where a suitable boat could be obtained at a reasonable charge.

Any other information which you think will help us would be very gratefully received.

- Continued -

ALL COMMUNICATIONS TO BE ADDRESSED TO "GENERAL SUPERINTENDENT"

GENERAL MANAGER & ENGINEER

TELEPHONE No. 41307.

General-Superintendent's Office,
Baths & Wash-houses Dept.,
Victoria Baths.
Sneinton. **Nottingham.**

J. T. GRUNDY, M.N.A.B-S
GENERAL SUPERINTENDENT

– Continued –

      On July 5th. a party will leave Nottingham
en-route to Belfast and I wonder if I may presume on your
good nature to either engage accommodation for us or inform
us where to write to.

      The party will require full board for a
fortnight, as follows:-

    3   Double Rooms.

    4   Single Rooms.

    Thanking you in anticipation.

          Yours faithfully,

          J. T. Grundy

          General Manager
            & Engineer.

with both day trippers and the many families from Belfast who
decamped *en masse* to rent any available properties in the town
for the whole of the summer. It could perhaps be argued that, as
the main holiday period in England would be in August rather
than July, this was a reasonable oversight. However, when taken
in conjunction with the earlier proposals to make the swim from
Larne to Stranraer, it does display a certain naïvety among Tom's
team and demonstrates just how much they would be relying on
local people's knowledge to ensure the success of the swim.

16th April 1947.

Mr. J.T. Grundy, M.N.A.B.S.,
Baths & Wash-houses Dept.,
Victoria Baths,
Sneinton, Nottingham.

Dear Sir,

Re yours of 10th inst.

I shall be very much i terested in the proposed attempt to swim
from Ireland to Scotland by Mr. Blower and shall be very pleased to
furnish you with any information, etc., that may be of any assistance
to further the success of the attempt. Miss Glietz had two pilots.
One of them is still living and I have no doubt would still be
available. His name is Andrew white and he resides in Moat Street,
Donaghadee. I have not seen him since receiving your letter but do
not anticipate you would have any trouble fixing up with him.

As regards accommodation. This will be a difficult matter. I
have been making several enquiries but as yet without success but will
let you know in the course of a day or two what further progress I
have been able to make. Accommodation is very difficult to obtain
here for the summer and is usually booked up a year ahead. Th

The tides and currents, both on this and the Scotch side, are
very deceiving and difficult. At the time of Miss Gleize's swim,
Mr. White was thought to be the best we could get and I am still of
this opinion. I might also add that he is coxswain of the Donaghadee
Lifeboat.

I am only sorry that the Government took away my boat during the
war and eventually lost it in a storm, otherwise it would have been
available to give you all the assistance required. I do not at the
moment know of another as suitable a boat but there will be plenty of
boates available to chose from and I do not anticipate any difficulty
in obtaining one to do the purpose.,

Hoping that the attempt meets with every success.

Yours faithfully.

The letters continued between the two men, the upshot of
which was that Tom, along with his immediate family and trainer, would take up residence in the Lighthouse Cafe, Donaghadee
while the remainder of his party would stay in Bangor.

After some negotiations Andy White, despite initially seem-
ingly reluctant, undertook to Pilot the attempt and also sup-

Andy White

ply a rowing boat with oarsmen. The terms of this employment would see White receive £40, whether or not the swim was successful, plus an undecided amount as a bonus, should the swim be successful!

The plan for the swim was that the rowing boat would act as a pilot boat / feed station just ahead of Tom, while a motor launch would travel alongside.

Mr Roberts' motor boat, *The Kathleen* had been pressed into service with the Admiralty during the war and during this service had unfortunately been lost in a storm. Roberts thus began to search for a suitable replacement as evidenced in his letter below.

Although the efforts of Mr Roberts in securing a pilot boat do not seem to have born fruit, Tom's team were also exploring various other avenues. These included an approach to the Admiralty asking that a Royal Navy Corvette be permitted to accompany Tom, for the duration of the swim but it was an equally fruitless effort as the *Nottingham Journal* reported on 5th June 1947:

NO CORVETTE FOR TOM BLOWER'S BIG SWIM

Tom Blower the Nottingham swimmer with a war record in corvettes, will not have a corvette to accompany him on his projected Irish Channel Swim

Mr James Harrison, M.P. for Nottingham East, has failed in his quest to the Admiralty that in recognition of Blowers distinguished service a corvette should be posted to help him in the swim in July.

Mr. Dugdal, Parliamentary Secretary to the Admiralty and M.P. for West Bromwich, told him that owing to the question of manpower (a corvette would require about 50 sailors) and the many difficulties of providing a crew and allocating a ship and the fact that if they established a precedent in the matter they would probably be approached by other sporting promoters, reluctantly they must refuse.

23rd May 1947.

Mr. John Cooper, Tug Owner,
155 Corporation Street,
BELFAST.

Dear Sir,

I have had communication with a Mr. Grundy from Nottingham who is acting as manager for the well-known channel swimmer Mr. Tom Blower, who proposes swimming from here to Port Patrick.

Mr. Grundy was advised to contact me as my motor cruiser had been used as a tender on the occasion when Miss Gleitze made the attempt. Unfortunately, I no longer possess a boat as mine was lost by the admiralty during the war. I suggested to Mr. Grundy that from my experience a tug would be the most suitable type of vessel for this purpose. As he is a stranger in these parts, he asked me if I could find a suitable vessel also the cost of hire. The attempt is to be made on the first suitable opportunity between the 12th July and the 24th July.

You might therefore let me know the terms which I will forward to Mr. Grundy, or perhaps you would rather make direct contact, in which case his address is Mr. Grundy, General Manager & Engineer, Baths & Wash-houses Dept., Victoria Baths, Sneinton, Nottingham.

I would point out that in the event of the swim being a success there will probably be prospects of several more attempts by those who have already swam the English Channel.

Thanking you in anticipation.

Yours faithfully.

One of Mr Roberts efforts to secure a
support boat for the swim

However an approach at official level to the Bangor Town Clerk, Mr R. M. Moore, by Alderman Ashworth of Nottingham was more successful.

On hearing of the request, Mr. J.B. Lamont of the Princetown Road in the town offered the use of his motor boat *The Morning Star* as reported in the *News Letter*. In a subsequent report Mr. Lamont made it clear that he was only too pleased to make his boat available *"to an Englishman with such a big heart"* for the swim and was confident of Tom's chances of success.

Thus as the date for Tom's swim approached, it seems that he was at the very peak of his powers. The previous 12 months had seen him train relentlessly and prepare himself thoroughly. Whilst by nature Tom was a very humble man, his preparations ensured he was confident that he had the North Sea Channel swim 'in him!'

On the 3rd July Tom left Nottingham to catch the Liverpool Ferry which would take them to Belfast. Travelling via the Liverpool Ferry, they would reach their Donaghadee HQ, the Lighthouse Cafe, the following day 4th July 1947.

The First Attempt

Tom Blower (right) surveys the North Channel with (l to r) his wife Clarice, son Michael, trainer C Craig and Mr George Ashe
Northern Whig 5th July 1947

From their arrival on Friday 4th July 1947, it appears there was a great warm welcome shown to Tom and his party. Evidently the town was buzzing with anticipation as expectancy grew day by day. Despite initial scepticism from some of the townsfolk which was reported in the *Nottingham Evening Post*, Tom's swimming prowess was evident for all to see and soon he was being treated by Donaghadee people as one of their own.

Tom and his immediate family took up residence in the Lighthouse Cafe. Ideally placed, the cafe (which was situated between Pier 36 and the lifeboat shop) overlooked the harbour and was only 20 yards from the sea. The only downside was that accommodation was limited and due to the size of Tom's entourage some of his party were put up in Bangor.

Tom quickly settled into his daily routine. The heavy training was now behind him, so it was simply a case of daily swims to acclimatise to the sea temperature. These daily swims became something of a spectacle, as reports indicate people came from near and far just to witness him swimming in and around the harbour area. However Tom didn't restrict himself to the harbour often venturing as far as the Copelands.

At the time, Tom's plans to swim the North Channel were highly newsworthy and, no doubt attracted by the potential good PR, The Under Secretary for Air and MP for Central Nottingham, Geoffrey de Freitas, joined Tom for of one of his training swims.

However de Feitas found the water temperature not to his liking and soon returned to the boat leaving Tom to complete the rest of his two hour training stint alone!

l-r: :CE Cragg (Trainer) Mr G de Freitas (Under Secretary for Air), Alderman R E Ashworth (Chairman of the Swim Committee), Tom Blower and Mr J. T. Grundy (Manager)
Belfast News Letter 7th July 1947

As previously explained to maximise the chances of success any attempt to swim the North Channel should be made as close as possible to a neap tide when tidal currents are at their weakest. Tom's arrival in Donaghadee on 4th July was timed to allow him a few days acclimatisation before the neap tide on 11th July.

However as well as a neap tide (which is predictable) a successful attempt also requires a favourable weather window of around 16 hours (which is not!) as explained in this interview with Tom's trainer, Mr Cragg in the *Nottingham Evening Post* on 10th July 1947:

Tom Blower and Geoffrey de Freitas in the Harbour
Belfast News Letter 7th July 1947

TOM BLOWER ENDS HIS TRAINING
Ready For The North Channel Attempt

The people of Donaghadee, who had expressed some doubt to the ability of Tom Blower to swim the North Channel from Donaghadee to Port Patrick, have changed their minds since seeing the Nottingham swimmer in action. They have been greatly impressed by the strength of his overarm stroke and with his speed in the water, and they now feel that he only requires favourable conditions to accomplish this difficult swim. They are little apprehensive regarding the currents which sweep the Channel at about 4½ knots, but Tom Blower and his trainer do not anticipate that this difficulty is unsurmountable. Our Donaghadee representative had a talk with Trainer Cragg this morning and he stated that Blower had finished his training and is now taking things easy. He had a walk along the pier and then retired to bed.

"All depends on the weather," he said, "and while the reports do not encourage us in the belief that the attempt will be made this week, we are still hoping. "

"You can believe me when I say that when we get a 18- hour calm we shall be away."

Tom is in top-hole form and is very keen. He was the guest of honour at a dinner in Bangor last night at which Ald. R. E. Ashworth, the ex-Lord Mayor of Nottingham, thanked the Mayor, Coun. W. McMillan, and other officials the council, for the motor boat 'Morning Star,' which will carry the official party, Mr. Andrew White, who will in charge the pilot boat and a number of Donaghadee residents for the help they had given the organising committee connected with the swim. Ald. Ashworth agreed that the weather would have to change very much if Tom was get a chance to-morrow, and the chances a change before the week-end were remote.

If they were so unfortunate, two other periods were open them, the end of the month or mid-August. Among' those who joined in the good wishes were Mr T R Millington and L. Hewitt, of Messrs. John Player and Sons. Cragg expressed the opinion to our representative that Tom will be helped by the buoyancy of the water, which is greater because of the salt. He also said that swimmer had now finished with receptions until after the swim.

Ultimately the final decision to go or not lay with the swim's nominated pilot, Andy White, who would be responsible for Tom's safety during the swim. The Coxswain of the Donaghadee Lifeboat, White was an experienced local seaman who had piloted Mercedes Gleitze during several of her attempts to swim the North Channel. Tom would be totally reliant on White's judgement, both to guide him through the vagaries of the tricky currents off the Ulster coastline and to accurately predict the weather conditions which would prevail during the 16 or so hours required for the swim.

One can imagine that the events of the 10th and 11th of July must have been incredibly frustrating for all involved – they were prepared and as ready as they could be yet, in White's judgement, the weather remained unsuitable.

With the openings to swim during this neap tide window closing fast, reading between the lines there appears to have been an element of pressure to get the swimmer underway. Tom and his party simply couldn't stay indefinitely; funds were limited and they all had lives, family and work to be going on with, back in England.

Tom Blower and Andy White r
Belfast News Letter
5th July 1947

With Sunday 13th being adjudged to be the last day with a suitable tide for the next two weeks, was Saturday the 12th July going to be a big day in Donaghadee for both Tom and those celebrating their Orange tradition, or would they have to wait until Sunday the 13th?

Amid the inevitable press frenzy and frustration, all Tom could do was wait and watch the weather which by late on the 11th was starting to look promising.

To assess whether conditions were right or not White himself went out into the channel at 10pm on the 11th night, just to see firsthand the prevailing conditions. He planned a further check at 5 am on the morning of the 12th before making his final determination for that morning.

Then, with all the 'checks and balances' carried out, the decision was finally made. Tom would embark on his attempt at 9am on Saturday the 12th of July.

The *Nottingham Evening Post* on 12th July reported that White had great confidence in Tom's ability to accomplish the swim. He

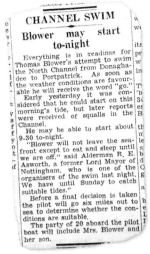

Belfast News Letter 11th July 1947 (left)
Nottingham Journal 11th July 1947 (right)

CHANNEL SWIM

Blower may start to-night

Everything is in readiness for Thomas Blower's attempt to swim the North Channel from Donaghadee to Portpatrick. As soon as the weather conditions are favourable he will receive the word "go."

Early yesterday it was considered that he could start on this morning's tide, but later reports were received of squalls in the Channel.

He may be able to start about 9.30 to-night.

"Blower will not leave the seafront except to eat and sleep until we are off," said Alderman R. E. Asworth, a former Lord Mayor of Nottingham, who is one of the organisers of the swim last night. We have until Sunday to catch suitable tides."

Before a final decision is taken the pilot will go six miles out to sea to determine whether the conditions are suitable.

The party of 20 aboard the pilot boat will include Mrs. Blower and her son.

BIG SWIM HELD UP

Blower Waits for Calm Spell

TOM BLOWER, the Nottingham swimmer, who is waiting at Donaghadee for favourable weather conditions which will enable him to make his bid to swim the North Channel, will not be able to make a start at 8.30 to-day, as he had hoped, owing to the squally weather, states Ald. R. E. Ashworth from Donaghadee.

"Our pilot," he said, "will take a trip in the morning at 6 o'clock to ascertain the condition of the waters a few miles out, so we may expect a chance to start with the next tide or on Saturday morning.

"We are all standing by waiting, with all preparations completed ready to start on the attempt. This is the hardest part of the job.

"We are spending every available minute on the sea front frequently inspecting the boat in which we intend to make the trip and which is tied up in the harbour.

"There is squally weather about, according to the Aldergrove R.A.F. weather report."

went on to explain that *"for the first three and a half hours Tom will have the assistance of the ebb tide before reaching the floods!"*

The plan was, that Tom would enter the water just behind the lighthouse, using the stonework's gentle slope to make his water entrance straightforward. Once in the water he would swim across, to what was known locally as the Wee Scotsman, a small outcrop of rock just off the south pier marked by an iron perch. If everything went to plan, this would be Tom's last touch of solid ground before swimming ashore in Scotland.

Blower May Start This Morning

"Quiet Sea" for Big Swim

TOM BLOWER, the Nottingham swimmer, hopes to start his North Channel swim about nine o'clock this morning.

A telephone message to the "Journal" from Donaghadee in the early hours of to-day gave the news that the pilot had been out after 10 p.m. and reported that while conditions were still not ideal, there had been an improvement.

The forecast was "changeable wind with quiet sea."

"As a final check the pilot plans to go out again at 5 a.m." it was stated.

Nottingham Journal 12th July 1947

On the morning of the 12th July, Donaghadee town was busy with townsfolk, holiday makers, sightseers, Orange Lodges and accompanying bands all happy to give the intrepid swimmer a rousing send off. Numerous accounts relate that huge crowds were waiting for Tom to appear on the harbour and one can only imagine the excitement and the sights and sounds that greeted Tom when he left his Hotel on the shore front to make his way down to the harbour. Certainly that particular Saturday morning. 'all roads led to the harbour at Donaghadee' as subsequently reported in the *Nottingham Journal* on 14th July:

BIG SEND OFF

Blower was given a tremendous send off when, well greased, smiling and looking exceptionally fit he started from the harbour behind the lighthouse.

Cars from far and near brought excited spectators to the coast. and motor boats did a roaring trade taking sightseers to the spot on the horizon where Blower was steadily breasting the waves.

Well over a dozen of them plied for hire circled the accompanying boats, cheering the intrepid swimmer on his way.

Followed by his team and supporters, and already covered in 'heat retaining grease', Tom purposefully made his way down to the back of the harbour area, near to the lighthouse. At 9:11am he slipped into the water to the sound of boisterous cheering and bands playing in the background. It would seem that the spectators may have been caught up in the excitement of the day, for newspaper reports indicate that very few, if any at all, gave thought to the possibility that the swim would be anything, other than a success!

Using his signature trudgeon[1] stroke and assisted by the ebbing tide which carried him away from the coast, Tom covered the first mile in half an hour and was reported to be going 'exceptionally well'

By midday Tom had been swimming for three hours and his support crew in the rowing boat passed him chicken broth in a bottle for his first feed. In the calm favourable conditions he had covered some 7½ miles, approximately one third of the way to Portpatrick.

---

1.   *Named after the English swimmer John Trudgen, the Trudgeon stroke, which was broadly used by Tom Blower during his successful North Channel swim, was an amalgam of swimming styles.*

The arms moved in a fashion that is similar to a contemporary freestyler but he leg movement was different. Rather than using the up down flutter kick of today, the Trudgeon stroke used a very simple scissors kick as many would still use when swimming on their sides.

The timing, or the ratio of strokes would be; one scissors movement of the legs for every two arm strokes.

THE CHANNEL SWIM

Blower starts this morning

THOMAS Blower will make his attempt to swim the North Channel from Donaghadee to Portpatrick to-day.

For a week he has been waiting for favourable weather. A forecast received late last night said that to-day the sea would be calm and the light wind would be from the south-west.

In these circumstances Andrew White, the pilot, decided that—unless there is a sudden change—Blower should start about 9 o'clock this morning.

Blower, whose stamina was proved when he swam the English Channel, is confident that he will succeed. He says that during the past week he has got accustomed to the cold water of the North Channel and that he expects to make the crossing in 12 or 13 hours.

He will wear a swim suit of fine silk, and will be thoroughly greased. He intends to use the trudgeon but will vary his stroke according to circumstances.

Mr. J. B. Lamont's motor boat, Morning Star, by which the official party will travel, will leave Bangor at 7 o'clock. She will carry provisions for 20 persons. When she reaches Donaghadee Blower will be waiting for her at the harbour and will have final consultations with Alderman R. E. Ashworth, a former Lord Mayor of Nottingham, who represents the promoters of the swim, the pilot and his trainer.

Mrs. Blower and her son will be in the official boat to cheer her husband, and to superintend the arrangements for feeding him as he swims.

There was a big crowd on the Donaghadee Pier early yesterday morning in the hope of seeing Blower take to the water, but Mr. Andrew White, who will be in charge of the pilot boat, decided, after going out to sea for several miles, on the postponement of the attempt.

Belfast News Letter 12th July 1947

Belfast News Letter
14th July 1947

By 12:30pm the tide had turned and rather than the ebb tide which had assisted him in swimming away from the County Down coast, Tom was now swimming in the Channel flood tide which brought with it a deterioration in the conditions. As the current became stronger, the sea grew increasingly choppy, the skies more overcast and Tom's progress had visibly slowed.

Despite this, in under 4 hours Tom had passed the point where Miss Gleitz had been forced to give up her attempt way back in the 1920s, a point it had taken her some 14 hours to reach.

Largely unaware of what was going on out in the channel, crowds were already gathering in Portpatrick in anticipation of celebrating a successful crossing and the Cross Keys Hotel, Tom's Scottish HQ, was made ready by its proprietor James Laird to greet the arrival of the intrepid swimmer.

Laird, in his younger days had himself been a noted swimmer and was an enthusiastic supporter of Tom. He was quoted in the *Nottingham Evening Post* on the 14th as saying that he had got Tom a *"bottle of his favourite ginger wine, which is the finest tonic*

for a man who has completed a long swim!" He went on to explain that this wine was extremely hard to come by and that it would be there waiting for the swimmer, no matter what time of the day or night he arrived!

"Only Blower's flashing arms could be seen as he left Donaghadee"

Belfast Newsletter 14/7/47

Unfortunately, any celebrations were premature.

As the conditions deteriorated and the tidal current strengthened, Tom's progress continued to slow. One of the observers in the support boat later said that for the last 2 hours he was in the water, Tom had been swimming hard, in an almost submerged state, to simply maintain position with no yardage being gained!

Swim Pilot Andy White on the tiller and Jim Kimm at the oars of the pilot Boat

Belfast Newsletter 14/7/47

Despite his gritty determination and an enormous desire to keep going, Tom eventually conceded and clambered unaided aboard the *Morning Star.* He had been persuaded by both Andy White and his trainer Mr. S E Cragg that the conditions were such, it would be impossible to reach the Scottish shore in the face of such a strong tide.

Thankfully though, they hadn't had *"tae pull him oot!"* Tom, on the advice of his pilot, had taken a very considered and wise decision that would later enable him to succeed in his challenge. That wisdom saw Tom remain so physically fresh, that the fol-

As the disappointing news eventually broke on both sides of the Channel. Perhaps the most notable reaction to the news is found in this press cutting from the Nottingham Journal 14th July 1947

lowing day he was up and back into the tide for a lengthy swim to simply 'loosen up!'

The *Nottingham Journal* dated 14th July describes how this attempt ended, in far more eloquent prose than I ever could, so I'll leave the last words on this unsuccessful Channel attempt to them:

"But sea and wind are stern and unrelenting adversaries, and when they act in concert even so stout a body as Blower's must give them best— temporarily at any rate!"

MAY WAIT A FORTNIGHT

THOMAS Blower will make another attempt to swim the North Channel from Donaghadee to Portpatrick.

He failed on Saturday because the wind freshened on the turn of the tide and in these areas it was impossible to make progress although he was prepared to continue swimming.

He entered the water at 9.11 a.m. and came out at 1.49 p.m., having been swimming steadily for 4 hours 38 minutes. He had covered approximately 12 nautical miles and was more than half-way to Portpatrick.

Not to-day

The neap tides will continue until to-morrow morning. The next neap tides are on July 26, 27 and 28. There is little likelihood of another attempt being made during the present neap tides. The weather report indicates that there will be a surface wind of about 15 knots to-day and that the sea would be choppy to-morrow.

Blower has been granted leave of absence by his firm, John Players & Sons, and should he have to wait until the next neap tides he will remain in Donaghadee.

Blower was so fresh on his return to Donaghadee that after a bath and a meal he went out for a walk along the sea front with his wife and eight-year-old son Michael, both of whom were in the official boat during the swim. Yesterday he had a five-mile practice swim.

The course

The course set on Saturday was to have taken three tides—north of Portpatrick on the ebb tide, south on the flood tide and then in to the Scottish coast swimming again in a northerly direction. It was reckoned that Blower would have to swim for about 14 hours to reach the Scottish coast.

He had been travelling so fast that his pilot, Andrew White, coxswain of the Donaghadee life-boat, estimated that Blower would have succeeded in between 10 and 11 hours had conditions remained favourable.

"Now that I know Blower's speed the swim can be planned for two tides instead of three," said White on the way back to Donaghadee.

Not exhausted

The swim took practically nothing out of Blower. During the last hour he had been battling against a heavy sea in which the yawl, used as a pilot boat, pitched and tossed so much that there was great difficulty in reaching food to the swimmer. There were times when the little boat was lifted up that it looked that it would crash down on his head as cups of chicken soup were being handed to him by his trainer. Mr. C. E. Cragg.

When White suggested the abandonment of the swim, Blower calmly treaded the water, and, in a normal voice, discussed the prospects with White, the officials, Alderman R. E. Ashworth and Mr. J. T. Grundy, and the owner of the motor launch, Mr. J. B. Lamont, of Bangor.

Blower wanted to continue, and it was only when White drew the pilot boat alongside that Blower gave up, remarking: "All right, I'll come in."

Unaided he pulled himself into the motor-boat. With a blanket wrapped round his waist and a towel over his shoulders, he went below deck and chatted freely, looking as fresh as he was at the end of his short practice swims.

The temperature of the sea at the start of the swim was 51 degrees and out in deep water it was down to 50.

Ready to start again

A "News-Letter" reporter, who watched the swim from the motor launch, had a talk with Blower shortly after he came out of the water. "The cold never troubled me," he said. "Any time I felt it I swam faster and, in fact, I don't even feel it now. I have done much longer stretches on practice swims and I am feeling perfectly fit, ready to go off again if we get a favourable weather report before the neap tides disappear.

White said: "I have not the slightest doubt about Blower swimming the North Channel under reasonable conditions, and I only insisted on his coming out of the water when I saw the hopelessness of the situation.

Perfect start

The weather conditions at the start of the swim were almost perfect. The wind was blowing lightly out of the south-west, the sea was calm and the sun shone brightly.

Good wishes were extended to Blower by Mr. J. A. Reid, on behalf of the Donaghadee Rugby Football Club, and Mr. C. M. Girvan, on behalf of the railway staff. Among the large crowd that had gathered was the Mayor of Bangor (Councillor W. H. M'Millan) and before Blower entered the water at the South Pier he was presented with a shamrock badge by Mrs. Millington, whose husband, Mr. P. B. Millington, with Mr. L. Hewett, represented John Players & Sons on the swim.

As soon as Blower started off the official party went on board the motor launch at the wheel of which was Mr. Ronald Lamont, son of the owner. Blower began at the rate of 22 strokes to the minute and when almost an hour out he had his first meal — malted milk and glucose. Six miles away was H.M.S. Howe heading for Bangor Bay.

The sea was now dead calm and the oarsmen in the pilot boat, Thomas Nelson and Samuel Kimm, were keeping nicely in front of Blower. A signal came back from the pilot boat that all was going well, and John Majury, who left 10 stone of dulce on the pier, to act as relief oarsman, remarked that Blower was swimming stronger and faster than Miss Mercedes Gleitz at any stage in her unsuccessful attempt several years ago.

Three miles in an hour

At the end of the first hour Blower was three miles out from Donaghadee and half a mile past the Copeland Islands. The Scottish coast was coming up clear and he was now well to the north of his Donaghadee-Portpatrick line swimming in the direction of Corsewell Point, at the southern entrance to Lough Ryan. He had increased his speed slightly to 23½ strokes to the minute and was travelling at about two miles an hour.

Mr. Lamont remarked: "If Tom Blower keeps at that speed he will be in Portpatrick in no time." A strong, warm sun was shining and the sky was cloudless overhead. Jackets, waistcoats and pullovers were being discarded by those in the official boat. One member was taking advantage of the glorious conditions to put in a spot of sun bathing.

Malted milk was prepared by Mrs. Blower in the galley of the official boat and was sent out by rowing boat to her husband. Holiday-makers were coming out from Donaghadee to see Blower. The motor-boats gave him a wide berth and the passengers cheered as they passed. Some called out: " Good luck, Tom, keep it going." One boat came a little too close and Blower was seen waving his arm to warn it off.

Where Miss Gleitz gave up

It was 12-11 p.m. and Blower had completed his third hour in the water. There was now no tide, and he was about 11 miles east of Black Head on the County Antrim coast. He was more than a third of the way, having covered approximately 7½ miles. Shortly afterwards he reached the point where Miss Gleitz gave up after being about 14 hours in the water. Blower's skin was a nice colour and he was not feeling the cold.

It was now 12-30 p.m. the start of the flood tide. Up to this Blower had been swimming north and different conditions were now setting in. He was meeting a one knot current to take him south. The current was to become gradually stronger in the next five or six hours.

The sea was becoming choppy. The sky was overcast and all discarded garments by those in the official party were being worn again.

White, who came on board the motor launch at 12-50 p.m. to take bearings, said that Blower was doing more than he expected. Blower shouted to the pilot boat: "By jove it's getting choppy." A heavy sea was beginning to run but he was still moving steadily.

Half-way

The wireless mast on the radio station at Portpatrick could be seen through glasses. The time was now 1-11 p.m. and Blower had been four hours in the water and had reached the half-way stage.

From then on it was a terrific struggle with Blower at times stroking as fast as 28 to the minute to keep himself on the course. Time and again he was carried off it. The wind became stronger and the waves higher until at 1-49 p.m. the final decision was made to abandon the attempt.

The Irish Amateur Swimming Association was represented by Mr. R. M'Ateer and Mr. C. Richardson.

Determination Brings Success

Although Tom's first attempt had been unsuccessful, when all the parties involved had metaphorically dusted themselves off and reviewed what had been achieved, the general consensus was that Tom had come tantalisingly close. With more favourable weather there was nothing that would cast any doubt on Tom's ability to ultimately succeed in his quest to conquer the channel.

Thus, having sought and been granted further time off from his work, Tom remained in Donaghadee aiming to make a second attempt at the earliest opportunity during the next neap tide, which would be in a six day window from 24th July.

By all accounts the family were well settled in Donaghadee and it appears that Tom had created a good impression with the local populace with his open, gentle and personable manner. As such, following that first attempt, the Donaghadee people had been delighted when they heard that he would remain in the town to give it another go during the next neap tide.

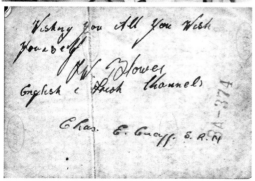

L to R: David Lindsay, Tom Blower, Morton McCauley and Andy Lindsay (the author's grandfather).

Tom kept in shape by swimming daily in and around the harbour area and during his 'down-time' mixed and socialised with both Donaghadee folk and the many tourists in the town.

Well informed rumour had it that Tom would make his second attempt on the first or second night of the neap tides but neither Thursday 24th nor Friday the 25th were suitable for various reasons.

However by Sunday 27th July an air of expectation in Donaghadee was palpable. It was no surprise then that when the town's Churches emptied after Evening Worship large crowds flocked to congregate at the harbour.

Around half past nine that Sunday night, Tom left his lodgings at The Harbour Cafe and made his way the short distance onto the South Pier. Such were the crowds however, that to avoid being mobbed he was transported by boat across to the North Pier, where he entered a small hut to change clothing and prepare himself. Then, at precisely 9:53 pm, Tom slipped into the flat calm water to huge cheers. Hundreds of onlookers and supporters were lining the South Pier using every available vantage point just to witness the start of this monumental swim.

Underlying Tom's quiet, easy-going exterior lay a deep conviction and a robust resolve to succeed in his 'mission' and that belief never wavered. It's recorded that when receiving a good luck kiss from his wife, prior to entering the water on the 27th he said to her, *"I'm not getting out for anybody this time."*

Above; Tom being rowed to the North Pier where he enters the water; below Photographs : J. Brown

Covered liberally in lanoline, (used to try to retain body heat) Tom swam gently across from the North Pier toward the South Pier where he touched the wall of the Harbour Mouth, just below the lighthouse. The *Northern Whig* recorded this event thus:

> He swam across from the pier and touched the harbour wall – a technicality to be completed under the rules of the swim – before setting off to sea.

Numerous newspaper accounts record that an armada of small boats, which were

Tom makes his way from the North Pier to the South Pier. Photograph: J. Brown

full of interested local people, accompanied the swimmer as he cleared the harbour although as time passed many of the accompanying boats slowly turned back home to Donaghadee.

Officially, Tom was to be accompanied by the motorboat *Morning Star* and one small rowing boat, which performed the role of pilot boat in front of him throughout the swim.

The *Morning Star* was described as being a 50 foot launch, owned and registered to a Mr. Lamont from Bangor whose son, Ronnie, was at the helm of the boat for the voyage

Some of the flotilla of boats which set out with Tom. Photograph: J. Brown

Aboard the launch and the rowing boat were a total of 22 people including; Mrs. Blower, Mr. Cragg (Tom's trainer), the ex Lord Mayor of Nottingham, two representatives from Tom's employers John Player and Sons, two representatives of the Irish Amateur Swimming Association, and four Donaghadee men who crewed the pilot boat – Andrew White (Donaghadee Lifeboat Coxswain and Tom's official Pilot for the swim), Jim Kimm (Engineer), Tom Simpson (weather man for the swim) and Billy Bassingthwaithe (Assistant Engineer).

Also mentioned as being aboard the *Morning Star* is Archie McVicker, an ex RUC Constable. A well known local swimmer, it was he who organised the Annual Copeland Island – Donaghadee Swim.

Tom touches the South Pier before striking out for Scotland
Photograph: J. Brown

As he commenced his swim leaving the harbour area and heading out toward the channel, it's recorded that Tom was using the trudgen stroke, at a rate of 22 strokes per minute.

One of the papers retelling of this story relates that there was hardly a ripple in the tide and that all the weather forecasts available, for the duration of the swim, were just about perfect with another source mentioning that:

> Shoals of herring at one time surrounded him so thickly that they nibbled his feet. The sea looked like a carpet of silver, and the pilot's boat propeller, churned up fish!"

Despite the apparently perfect conditions, not everyone was happy. Tom's wife later related how she had strong feelings of 'disquiet' regarding the weather saying, *"The Sea looked smooth, but it was a sort of slimy smoothness. And the sky was too red."* Little did she know!

Hourly updates on Tom's progress were communicated, via the *Belfast Telegraph*. The first at 10:53pm, (exactly one hour into the swim) read:

> 10:53pm – Swimming strongly, Blower is using the same course as he did on his first swim. Motorboats are plying between the shore and the swimmer.

The next 3 hourly updates simply reiterate his progress, charting that at 11:53pm he had travelled 6 miles and that darkness had fallen. An hour later Tom took his first meal, a quantity of malted milk which was prepared by his wife on the *Morning Star's* cooker, then conveyed to the swimmer by the men on the rowing boat. Whilst taking his food, Tom appeared fresh and chatted to both Andy White and to his trainer.

At 1:53am it is noted that Tom increased his speed and was now 11 miles out of Donaghadee.

By the time of the next report it would appear that some of Tom's well wishers had seen enough as the *Telegraph* dispatch reported:

> 2.53am. "Keep right on to the end of the road," sings one party returning to Donaghadee in a motor boat. Donaghadee light has almost disappeared.

In a separate press account of the events, it's recorded that the Scottish coast was sighted at 4 am and that by 4:53 am he was only 6.5 miles short of his target.

Returning to the hourly updates, the 3:53am, 4:53am and 5:53am despatches are all quite similar, reiterating what had been previously said. Tom was showing no signs of fatigue, taking another meal and each update separately mentions, confidently, that it appears he is well on course to be the first man to successfully make the swim!

However it is noted that just after the 5:53am update there was *"a light wind out of the North East (and it was) freshening."* although at the time this wasn't a major concern as it was blowing with the tide.

Whilst enjoying one of his brief stops for food, this time bread and jam along with his malted milk, Tom appeared in an optimistic mood, even exchanging jokes with the members of the official party. Greeting them with a cheery *"Good Morning"* he asked if they had slept well. When they responded in the negative he replied, *"I haven't had a wink of sleep myself!"* By this stage it is noted that most of the heat retaining grease/lanoline had been washed off his body.

Moving off again the water had calmed slightly and he made good headway into the North Current, which should sweep him toward the Scottish coast.

Back again to the *Telegraph* updates:

> 6:53am Lightning flashes across the sky, lighting up the Scottish coast. Will the weather beat him after he has gone so far?

The hourly *Belfast Telegraph* updates then appear to stop until 11:53 am but fortunately for posterity other newspapers recorded what occurred during those missing 5 hours.

Having swum for 8 hours in what can only be described as almost perfect conditions, the Channel had now changed into what experienced modern day swim pilot from Donaghadee Quinton Nelson describes on the Lone Swimmer Website as a sea with *"a fearsome reputation for chewing up and spitting out swimmers"* One news cutting records that:

> ... for the remainder of the time, it was a terrific battle against the elements. The conditions were awful and Blower's courage and endurance were magnificent.

Tom's coach, Mr. Cragg, reflected on the sudden change in weather and how it affected the swim saying *"no other man in the world could have done it – Tom just went plodding on, climbing up waves and sliding down on the other side!"*

Cragg explained that at the time, not one of the 22 people on the boats felt that Tom would make the finish. He further said that whilst they tried to smile and look upbeat for Tom, they all actually felt forlorn; sensing the ominous thoughts each other were having.

After being buffeted by heavy seas, gale force winds, thunderstorms and hailstones for more than 7 hours, Tom's body was looking somewhat the worse for wear. He no longer had full use of his left arm, he had damaged a ligament in his right leg, and his body was battered and heavily bruised. However Tom never once complained, remaining resolute that he would indeed finish the swim and although by this point, some wanted to take him from the water, Tom's wife, obeying his earlier instructions would not allow them.

One cutting stated;

> The wind now became stronger and the sea rougher. Conditions had changed completely. It was becoming a terrific battle against white capped waves. The pilot-boat was bobbing up and down like a cork. For a brief spell Blower changed from the trudgen to the breast stroke. The sea was actually worse than when it was decided to abandon the first attempt!
>
> News Letter 29th July

In an attempt to encourage Tom, one of the two observers from the Irish Amateur Swimming Association who was aboard the *Morning Star*, stripped and dived in to swim alongside Tom for an hour. However when he came out of the sea he was so cold that he had to thaw out his feet by putting them, wrapped in a blanket, inside the boat's oven!

The Pilot-Boat was being pitched and tossed around by the waves and Tom was now swimming simply to hold his position, being unable to gain any distance against the rampant tide – but crucially he wasn't losing ground.

And still the weather deteriorated.

When, sometime later, the Coxswain of the Portpatrick Lifeboat was asked about the weather on that day, he was to say that *"it was the worst storm and the worst water, he had seen for a long time"* How Tom remained in the water was beyond the understanding of all those watching.

One reporter later reflected, *"An hour earlier, his chances of success were 100-1 on, now they were 100-1 against!"* However, despite this gloomy prognosis others on the boat noted that between their position and the now visible Scottish coast, there appeared to be a stretch of more moderate water. If only Tom could push through and reach that calmer patch!

Having lost the *Belfast Telegraph* updates at 6:53 am, those in Northern Ireland would have been unaware of the drama that was unfolding in those long hours of silence but at 11:53 am the dispatches resumed. Although somewhat negative in candour, the update, simply gave details of Tom's current position, and went on to say that they believed that:

> "Blower still has 6 hours swimming to do before he reaches land."

An hour later at the 12:53pm update, it focused for the most part on the adverse weather, but by the 1:53pm dispatch it appears the prevailing mood was a lot brighter:

> The shore is only a stone's throw away from the Morning Star. Yes, it's almost certain he will make it. Still ploughing on without the slightest sign of fatigue.

Then, finally at 2:09 the history making news finally broke:

> It's all over. Blower is in Scotland. He has swum the Channel, better still he is the first person to accomplish this.

The press record of those final minutes, relate that the sun eventually shone as Tom:

> … entered a cove, as if in welcome, and to assure him that nature can be kind occasionally!"

As Tom finally came limping ashore the first man to clasp his hand was a Scottish policeman. *"You're the first one to do it, lad,"* he said, *"and you'll be the last."*

As we now know the Channel has since been crossed on many occasions. But that statement helps us to appreciate the enormity of Tom's achievement.

That final scene in this drama had been witnessed by the crew of two Scottish fishing boats, which had been travelling to the Isle of Man. Both crews stopped their boats, before clapping and cheering Tom as he finally touched Scottish land.

In closing this part of the story, I again turn to the online article in *Lone Swimmer* for this paragraph:

> "As he swam into a small Scottish cove the sky seemed to clear. He climbed agonizingly out of the water onto the rocks, and raised his clasped hands, shyly, above his head. "I can't tell anybody how I felt," said Clarice Blower. "I'd been every yard of the way with him in my mind. I just burst into tears with joy. But when I looked round everybody else was crying—21 men and me, one woman." It had taken Tom Blower 15 hours and 26 minutes to make the historic swim."
>
> Lone Swimmer Website

Return to Donaghadee

Given the excitement following Tom's triumph it is perhaps unsurprising that there are slight differences in how the press at the time recorded the events. One report states that the *Morning Star "arrived back in Donaghadee Harbour, late on Monday Night."* while another account along with photographs relates that the *Morning Star* with Tom on board made a triumphant entry into Donaghadee harbour, in broad daylight at 1:15pm on the Tuesday afternoon!

The Belfast Telegraph reported on the evening of the 28th:

THE NORTH CHANNEL SWIM MADE

23 Miles in 15 Hours 27 Mins. .

"He's done it." shouted the crowd at Portpatrick to-day when it was announced that burly Tom Blower, the Nottingham tobacco factory worker, had reached the Scottish shore at 1.20 p.m., and was the first man ever to cross the North Channel between Donaghadee and Portpatrick – about 23 miles.

HANDICAPS OVERCOME.

It took 15 hrs. 27 mins. to attain his object. He entered the water at 9.53 p.m. on Sunday, overcame shoals of herring, a thunderstorm and bitterly cold water. Although suffering from bruises Blower looked "as fit as fiddle" when seen in his Portpatrick hotel. This was his second attempt to cross the tricky stretch of water. On July 12 heavy seas compelled him to accept defeat when he had been over four hours out from Donaghadee.

WANTS TO TRY OTHER WAY.

Blower has another object in view. He wants to swim the North Channel from Portpatrick to Donaghadee. Fishermen told a "Belfast Telegraph" reporter that this could be an even more hazardous swim than the present one. This swim, however, will not be attempted for some time. When the Donaghadee lifeboat received the news of Blower's success. a miniature "Hampden" roar went up from the hundreds of holidaymakers and townspeople who had gathered.

Fog will probably prevent the swimmer and his party returning to Ulster this evening.

However there is a very simple explanation to this apparent ambiguity.

On completion of his swim Tom clambered aboard the *Morning*

Star, which then made haste to Portpatrick Harbour. Arriving around 3pm that Monday afternoon, Tom left the boat, went ashore and made his way, slowly due to the large crowds of well-wishers, to The Cross Keys Hotel (His Scottish Headquarters) where he spent the night.

Whilst Tom spent that evening washing himself down, recovering and no doubt celebrating in the comfort of Mr Laird's Hotel, the *Morning Star* left Portpatrick and returned to Donaghadee. Then the following morning they returned to pick Tom up, before again making their way back to Donaghadee Harbour. It's reported that whilst departing Portpatrick a large crowd of spectators bade Tom farewell by giving him a hearty rendition of, *'Will Ye no come back again.'*

Certainly the photographs of the small flotilla of boats and their arrival into the harbour in broad day light, leave no doubt, that Tom's actual triumphant return to Donaghadee, on board the *Morning Star* was at 1:15pm on Tuesday 29th July.

Some of the flotilla of boats the returned with Tom to Donaghadee including the Morning Star (centre)

Belfast News Letter 30th July 1947

A contemporary press cutting gives us an idea of the reception which awaited the history making swimmer in Donaghadee:

Donaghadee harbour was the scene of great animation this morning in anticipation of the arrival of Tom Blower, the North Channel swimmer.

When almost three miles out Blower and the party from the other side were met by a fleet of heavily laden motor boats and other craft whose occupants cheered him wildly and sang 'For he's a Jolly Good Fellow,' and 'Bring Back my Tommy to me.'

On the pier head there were thousands of people assembled and when Blower's launch entered the harbour at 1:15 the cheering was renewed, while two lifeboat rockets were fired in token of welcome.

There are various press cuttings recording Tom's return to Donaghadee, all of which convey scenes of wonderful celebrations!

The Headline in the *Belfast News Letter* 30th July was:

BLOWER RETURNS TO DONAGHADEE

Great Reception after North Channel Swim

The article detailed that the *Morning Star* was escorted into Donaghadee by no less than 14 Motor Boats, which contained about 800 people (no health and safety issues back then!) and went on to say:

> On this side one of the craft to greet the Morning Star was a speed boat from Bangor which fell in beside the launch three miles from Donaghadee. It was packed with people who cheered Blower again and again as he waved to them.
>
> Meanwhile every pleasure craft from Donaghadee, fully dressed with bunting and flags, had put out from the harbour. When they reached the launch they took up positions to port and starboard and astern. Thus escorted, the Morning Star, with Blower on deck acknowledging

the cheers, entered the harbour. The life-boat gun fired two rockets from the pier, and it was a signal for a roar from the crowd which never stopped until the swimmer had reached his hotel.

Tom was officially presented with a garland of laurel leaves, tied with red, white and blue ribbons by Chairman of the Donaghadee Urban Council Mrs. J Boyd, M.B.E., J.P. and further officials congratulated Tom on his success before he himself said a few words of thanks to the people of Donaghadee, for all the kindness shown to him.

The *Belfast Telegraph* reported that it took:

> ... almost a quarter of an hour to get from the lighthouse to the end of the pier, so dense was the throng. Hundreds shook hands with him, and one enthusiastic old lady put her arms round his neck and kissed him, much to Blower's embarrassment.

To the victor the laurels,

Belfast News Letter
30th July 1947

Fortunately local policemen including Archie McVicker, who had been onboard the *Morning Star* during the swim, eventually managed to make a passage-way and got Tom to sanctuary.

Even then Tom hadn't exhausted the frenzied crowd, as they simply followed the swimmer down to his hotel and once there a loud chant of *"We Want Blower!"* arose!

In response, one of Tom's party, Mr. Ashworth the ex Lord Mayor of Nottingham, opened an upstairs window to address the crowd. Again he thanked the Ulster people for their wonderful co-operation and assistance. Going on, he said that they'd had a marvellous reception in Portpatrick, but it was nothing to what the Donaghadee people were doing.

Still unsatisfied, the crowd continued to shout for Tom and finally the swimmer appeared at the open window. He articulated his own personal indebtedness to all those who had helped him.

It would appear that, having heard from Tom, the crowd, now satisfied, dispersed somewhat. However that wasn't the end of the revelry, not by a long shot!

The remainder of that afternoon and early evening saw Tom, his wife Clarice and their son travel over to Bangor. Whilst the reason is not recorded as such, it's not a huge leap to assume that they wanted get away from the crowds but, if that was the case, it wasn't entirely successful.

Returning to their Donaghadee Headquarters at 11pm that Tuesday night at the end of a long tiring day, the Blowers must surely have been astounded when, according to newspaper reports, they found themselves faced with, *'a procession, headed by the Ballyfrenis Accordion Band.'* Many within the huge crowd carried flags and placards. Inscriptions included, *'Hail Victor!'* *'Hats off to Blower'* *'The Channel Conqueror'* and *'Cheers to Tom Blower, from Donaghadee!'*

Tom, his family and his trainer were then:

> … lifted into a gaily decorated motor car and accompanied by the band, with a large gathering of people, were taken on a triumphal tour of the town. In East Street the car was stopped by the dense throng, and Blower had to make a short speech
>
> Belfast Telegraph 3rd July 1947

Sometime after midnight the party eventually wound its way back to their hotel, where Tom yet again addressed the crowd from an upstairs window. He stated that he had never seen such a display of enthusiasm in his life, before retiring for the night.

The following evening (Wednesday) saw a more formal celebration of Tom's achievement when the Donaghadee Urban Council hosted an official celebratory supper in his honour at the Town Hall.

Those fortunate enough to be present included many officials from the local Council, dignitaries from Nottingham City Council, representatives of Tom's employers John Players, representatives of the Irish Amateur Swimming Association and the four local men who had crewed the Pilot boat. Tom and his party were welcomed to the event by a guard of honour, which was formed by the local Sea Rangers.

Amongst the many congratulatory messages one in the form of a telegram from the then Northern Ireland Prime Minister, Sir Basil Brooke was read out. In it Brooke simply said that he wanted to convey to Tom, *"his heartiest congratulations, on his magnificent achievement!"*

During the evening a bouquet of flowers plus a cheque for £141 was presented to Mrs. Blower, as a gift from the townspeople of Donaghadee in appreciation of her husband's magnificent achievement. In response Mrs. Blower said that she wasn't able to put into words how she felt but went on to say, *"I think I am the proudest woman in Ireland tonight and one of the luckiest, don't you? I think you all love Tom – and I do too!"*

During the evening, a large crowd of well-wishers gathered out-side the building. In response Tom made several visits to open windows overlooking the crowd. One of the newspaper cuttings observed that, speaking out the window, Tom made what was *"a very happy speech"* saying *"One thing he liked about Donaghadee was that everybody knew everybody else, and that although he had only been there a month, already he seemed to know everybody."* Going on, he made it clear that very soon he would return for a holiday and this was greeted by renewed cheering.

Others also spoke to the crowd from the open upstairs window, but perhaps the biggest cheer of the night, outside those for Tom himself, were saved for Andy White and Tom Simpson, two of Donaghadee's own, who had played such a vital part in the suc-cessful swim. Tom Simpson explained that unless you had been there to see them, no one could conceive the conditions Tom had to contend with, especially in the last 4 hours of the swim. It was his belief that there was not another man in the world who could emulate Tom Blower's feat.

Concluding the public proceedings everyone sang the National Anthem before what the papers describe as *"three cheers and a 'Donaghadee whisper' for Tom Blower."*

Afterwards whilst still in the Town Hall, the invited guests made their way downstairs where supper was to be served. One of the press cuttings articulates:

> Supper was served in the cafe downstairs, and the informal atmos-phere was greatly enjoyed by everyone. Mr. Blower regaled those present with humorous anecdotes and songs were sung by Mrs. Giovanelli, Mrs. Thompson, Miss Nelson, Mr. Kimm and Mr. Tommy Simpson.

Further gifts were presented to Mrs. Blower, by Miss Peggy Clarke on behalf of the Donaghadee Sea Rangers who, at one point in the evening's proceedings, provided Tom with a 'Guard of Honour'. Subsequently, and to conclude the evening, everyone then joined in with singing a hearty rendition of *'For he's a Jolly Good Fellow.'*

It is interesting to note that while the various newspaper reports of the time are in broad agreement about the events of the evening there is some disagreement as to their precise sequencing and indeed location, with some reports suggesting that the Lighthouse Cafe was the epicentre of much of the action. Perhaps the reporters weren't invited to witness events first hand or perhaps they were and got too involved in the celebrations leading to reduced powers of recollection!

The following day, Thursday, saw Tom and his party pack up for their journey home to Nottingham. Once more a large crowd turned up to say good-bye to Tom at the town's railway station.

Amazingly though, this didn't appear to satisfy the Donaghadee folk who refused to let this be their 'last farewell.' The *Belfast Telegraph* describes events that took place later that Thursday evening:

> About 10:30 on Thursday night boat-loads of people went out into the Channel and met the Liverpool boat on which Blower was travelling back to England. They cheered the swimmer lustily, and further greeting was in the shape of rockets which were fired from the pier at Donaghadee Harbour.

I think it's fair to say, that the local Donaghadee people appeared to have had an insatiable desire to see and spend time with Tom, who by now was being regarded as a 'local' hero.

This chapter detailing the events following Tom's conquering of the North Channel may seem quite long but it needs to be to recount the extent of the celebrations which ensued.

It seems clear from the extensive celebrations that the Donaghadee and Portpatrick people accorded Tom the level of adulation a sports man or woman would get today on their return from having claimed a major world championship title.

The residents of these two ports facing each other across the North Channel were very familiar with the challenges the short stretch of water between them presented to anyone daring to swim across its icy depths and it's fair to say that they were awed by Tom's achievement.

In recent times the North Channel has been conquered by a select band of swimmers who have been able to draw on modern methods of training and conditioning in preparation for the challenge. But back in 1947 such things were unheard of and the views of those familiar with the North Channel were concisely voiced by the policeman who greeted Tom when he emerged from the water on the Scottish coast when he said *"You're the first one to do it, lad – and you'll be the last."*

Home Again

Finally then, Tom had left Donaghadee and Northern Ireland behind him, however as it turned out his time in the spotlight wasn't quite over!

On returning to his home city of Nottingham, he learned that he was to be honoured by the people of the City, at a Civic Reception in the formal surroundings of the Council House. The reception was well attended, the guest list including such 'luminaries' as, The Nottingham Lord Mayor and The Sheriff of Nottingham. Also in attendance were the four men from Donaghadee who had crewed the Pilot Boat during Tom's swim.

The evening commenced when an inscribed, 130 year old Silver Cup was presented to Tom by the Council to commemorate the history making Swim. They further gave Tom the 'written log' of the Swim, which had been kept on the day by his Coach.

Responding Tom thanked the Council for their support, before again expressing his gratitude to the people of Northern Ireland.

In extending an official welcome to the four Donaghadee men a special mention was made of Donaghadee Lifeboat Coxswain Mr. Andrew White who had been Tom's pilot throughout the swim. One Council Official described White as being, *"The King of Donaghadee, who knew every ripple of the Channel!"*

Responding, White described Tom as a *"Gladiator, who had won a terrific battle with nature!"*

During their visit, the Donaghadee party took the opportunity to visit the Nottingham Lido which Tom had used extensively in his training for the North Channel swim. At one point in his preparation he had actually stayed swimming in the Lido for 16 long hours!

This 'dropping by' the Lido was no accident as several news clippings report that the journey made to Nottingham by the Donaghadee men had another purpose as well as representing Donaghadee at the official function.

> "The other (reason for going to Nottingham) was to take notes on
> the general lay-out of the lido and particularly the children's pool, for
> Donaghadee has ideas about a children's pool as a war memorial.
>
> Nottingham Journal 6th September 1947

Sadly for the children of Donaghadee it appears that this part
of the visit bore no fruit!

Visit to Bulwell Lido,
where Tom trained and
made his first practice
swims of 16 hours. L
to R. Tom Blower, Andy
White, C.E. Cragg, W.
Bassingthwaighte, J.T.
Kimm, Tom Simpson.

Tom Blower's long distance swimming adventures continued
after the momentous events of 1947 with attempts on 'there
and back' double crossings of the English Channel in 1948 and
1951. However it will be for his success in conquering the North
Channel that Tom will be most fondly remembered.

During one interview with the press after the North Channel
success, Tom's wife Clarice is quoted as saying of her husband,
"They get the bug, and it kills them in the end."

Unfortunately, with hindsight, this almost glib remark appears
to have been prophetic.

No one can tell whether regularly driving himself to the outer limits of human endurance was a contributory factor in Tom's final demise. But whatever the cause, at home on the 17th February 1955 Tom suffered a heart attack which proved fatal and, at just 41 years of age, he was gone.

His mighty heart, which had powered him through countless swimming adventures in the end gave up and failed him.

Perhaps a fitting epitaph to Tom would be a remark made to him in 1951 by Florence Chadwick, a world renowned American Channel Swimmer, who went on to set many long distance swimming records.

Tom had just been pulled from the English Channel whilst unsuccessfully attempting to swim it both ways and, after returning to the shore at Calais, was met by Chadwick who exclaimed

"You are the Greatest Swimmer alive today!"

An appropriate tribute.

Dear Reader,

I hope you have enjoyed this publication from Ballyhay Books, an imprint of Laurel Cottage Ltd. We publish an eclectic mix of books ranging from personal memoirs to authoritative books on local history, from sport to poultry, from photographs to fiction and from music to marine interests – but all with a distinctly local flavour.

To see details of these books, as well as the beautifully illustrated books of our sister imprint Cottage Publications, why not visit our website **www.cottage-publications.com** or telephone +44 (0)28 9188 8033.

Timothy S Johnston

BALLYHAY BOOKS